ADVISER, TEACHER, ROLE MODEL, FRIEND

ON BEING A MENTOR TO STUDENTS IN SCIENCE AND ENGINEERING

NATIONAL ACADEMY OF SCIENCES
NATIONAL ACADEMY OF ENGINEERING
INSTITUTE OF MEDICINE

NATIONAL ACADEMY PRESS
Washington, D.C. 1997

NATIONAL ACADEMY PRESS • 2101 Constitution Ave., N.W. • Washington, DC 20418

NOTICE: This volume was produced as part of a project approved by the Governing Board of the National Research Council, whose members are drawn from the councils of the National Academy of Sciences, the National Academy of Engineering, and the Institute of Medicine. It is a result of work done by the Committee on Science, Engineering, and Public Policy (COSEPUP) as augmented, which has authorized its release to the public. This report has been reviewed by a group other than the authors according to procedures approved by COSEPUP and the Report Review Committee.

The **National Academy of Sciences** (NAS) is a private, nonprofit, self-perpetuating society of distinguished scholars engaged in scientific and engineering research, dedicated to the furtherance of science and technology and to their use for the general welfare. Under the authority of the charter granted to it by Congress in 1863, the Academy has a working mandate that calls on it to advise the federal government on scientific and technical matters. Dr. Bruce M. Alberts is president of the NAS.

The **National Academy of Engineering** (NAE) was established in 1964, under the charter of the NAS, as a parallel organization of distinguished engineers. It is autonomous in its administration and in the selection of members, sharing with the NAS its responsibilities for advising the federal government. The National Academy of Engineering also sponsors engineering programs aimed at meeting national needs, encourages education and research, and recognizes the superior achievements of engineers. Dr. William A. Wulf is president of the NAE.

The **Institute of Medicine** (IOM) was established in 1970 by the NAS to secure the services of eminent members of appropriate professions in the examination of policy matters pertaining to the health of the public. The Institute acts under the responsibility given to the NAS in its congressional charter to be an adviser to the federal government and, on its own initiative, to identify issues of medical care, research, and education. Dr. Kenneth I. Shine is president of the IOM.

The **Committee on Science, Engineering, and Public Policy** (COSEPUP) is a joint committee of the NAS, the NAE, and the IOM. It includes members of the councils of all three bodies.

Financial Support: The development of this guide was supported by the Robert Wood Johnson Foundation and the Burroughs-Wellcome Fund. Dissemination support for this guide was provided by the American Mathematical Society.

Internet Access: This report is available via World Wide Web at http://www.nap.edu/readingroom/books/mentor.

Order from: National Academy Press, 2101 Constitution Ave., N.W., Washington, DC 20418. *Pricing:* 1 copy, $7.95; 2–9 copies, $6.50 each; and 10 or more copies, $4.95 each. All orders must be prepaid with delivery to a single address. Prices are subject to change without notice. To order by credit card, call 1-800-624-6242 or 202-334-3313 (in Washington metropolitan area).

International Standard Book Number: 0-309-06363-9

Cover illustration by Leigh Coriale.

Printed in the United States of America

COMMITTEE ON SCIENCE, ENGINEERING, AND PUBLIC POLICY

PROJECT GUIDANCE GROUP

DAVID R. CHALLONER *(Chair)*, Vice President for Health Affairs, University of Florida

ELLIS B. COWLING, University Distinguished Professor At-Large, North Carolina State University

MILDRED DRESSELHAUS, Institute Professor of Electrical Engineering and Physics, Massachusetts Institute of Technology

MARIAN KOSHLAND, Professor of Immunology, Department of Molecular and Cell Biology, University of California, Berkeley

MARY J. OSBORN, Department of Microbiology, University of Connecticut Health Center

WILLIAM JULIUS WILSON, Lucy Flower University Professor of Sociology and Public Policy, University of Chicago

Principal Project Staff

DEBORAH D. STINE, Project Director
ALAN ANDERSON, Consultant-Writer
PATRICK P. SEVCIK, Research Associate
LYNNE GILLETTE, Staff Officer
NORMAN GROSSBLATT, Editor

iv

PREFACE

This guide—intended for faculty members, teachers, administrators, and others who advise and mentor students of science and engineering—attempts to summarize features that are common to successful mentoring relationships. Its goal is to encourage mentoring habits that are in the best interests of both parties to the relationship. While this guide is meant for mentoring students in science and engineering the majority of it is widely applicable to mentoring in any field.

This guide is descended from a series of related publications. The original concept grew out of the Committee on Science, Engineering, and Public Policy (COSEPUP) report *Reshaping the Graduate Education of Scientists and Engineers* (1995), which showed that students need to be flexibly prepared for a range of careers and urged that graduate education be revised so as to prepare students better for productive and satisfying careers. (See Addendum.)

Discussions during and after the preparation of *Reshaping* indicated the need for a guide for students who are planning their education and professional careers. The guide that emerged, *Careers in Science and Engineering: A Student Planning*

Guide to Grad School and Beyond (1996), sought to help students take a broader view of the potential applications of their science and engineering education. A related student guide, which considers questions of ethics and scientific integrity, is *On Being a Scientist: Responsible Conduct in Research* (1995).

In the process of developing *Careers*, graduate and postdoctoral students in focus groups noted that faculty and advisers needed guidance as well to adapt to changing employment conditions. This guide is meant to complement *Careers* by assisting mentors and advisers in understanding how they might help students identify and respond to the challenges of becoming scientists or engineers. For convenience, the text contains several types of boxes:

- ➤ Tips: Steps to improve mentoring.
- ➤ Styles: Examples of poor and good mentoring.
- ➤ Facts: The context of mentoring.
- ➤ Profiles: A sample of nonacademic careers, from *Careers in Science and Engineering: A Student Planning Guide to Grad School and Beyond.*
- ➤ Summary points: Chapter summaries.

COSEPUP has also developed a sample form to help evaluate faculty mentors. The form can be adapted by individual institutions to suit their own needs. The version of the form offered here is most appropriate for use by advanced graduate students (for example, third-year and higher PhD students), postdoctoral fellows, and recent doctoral-program graduates who have had a long relationship with a mentor. The book and the form are both at the following Web address: http://www.nap.edu/readingroom/books/mentor. See "Mentoring" under "Resources" for further discussion of assessment methods.

ACKNOWLEDGMENTS

The preparation of this guide was overseen by a guidance group consisting of David Challoner (chair), Ellis Cowling, Mildred Dresselhaus, Marian Koshland, Mary Osborn, and William Julius Wilson.

Valuable feedback was provided by an external advisory group composed of Douglas Bodner, George Campbell Jr., Carlos Gutierrez, Karen Harpp, Susan Kiehne, Susan Lasser, Susan Mims, Norine Noonan, Richard Tapia, and Michael Zigmond. Special thanks go to Beth Fischer and Michael Zigmond for excellent references, Martha Shumate Absher for information on students with disabilities, and Marjorie Olmstead for her article on mentoring junior faculty.

Three focus groups, attended by some four dozen faculty and students from 16 colleges and universities, gathered for helpful and spirited discussions of this guide in Washington, DC, at Sigma Xi in Research Triangle Park, NC, and at the California State University, Long Beach. Thanks go to Lynne Gillette, Ellis Cowling, Stuart Noble-Goodman, and Glenn Nagel for recruiting the focus groups.

Staff for the project included Deborah Stine, associate director of COSEPUP and project director; Lynne Gillette, staff officer on temporary assignment from the Department of Energy; Alan Anderson, science writer; Norman Grossblatt, editor; and Patrick Sevcik, research associate.

CONTENTS

LIST OF BOXES

CONTENTS

xi

1

WHAT IS A MENTOR?

The notion of mentoring is ancient. The original Mentor was described by Homer as the "wise and trusted counselor" whom Odysseus left in charge of his household during his travels. Athena, in the guise of Mentor, became the guardian and teacher of Odysseus' son Telemachus.

In modern times, the concept of mentoring has found application in virtually every forum of learning. In academics, *mentor* is often used synonymously with *faculty adviser*. A fundamental difference between mentoring and advising is more than advising; mentoring is a personal, as well as, professional relationship. An adviser might or might not be a mentor, depending on the quality of the relationship. A mentoring relationship develops over an extended period, during which a student's needs and the nature of the relationship tend to change. A mentor will try to be aware of these changes and vary the degree and type of attention, help, advice, information, and encouragement that he or she provides.

In the broad sense intended here, a mentor is someone who takes a special interest in helping another person develop into a successful professional. Some students, particularly those working in large laboratories and institutions, find it difficult to develop a close relationship with their faculty adviser or laboratory director. They might have to find their mentor elsewhere—perhaps a fellow student, another faculty member, a wise friend, or another person with experience who offers continuing guidance and support.

In the realm of science and engineering, we might say that a good mentor seeks to help a student optimize an educational experience, to assist the student's socialization into a disciplinary culture, and to help the student find suitable employment. These obligations can extend well beyond formal schooling and continue into or through the student's career.

The Council of Graduate Schools (1995) cites Morris Zelditch's useful summary of a mentor's multiple roles: "Mentors are advisors, people with career experience willing to share their knowledge; supporters, people who give emotional and moral encouragement; tutors, people who give specific feedback on one's performance; masters, in the sense of employers to whom one is apprenticed; sponsors, sources of information about and aid in obtaining opportunities; models, of identity, of the kind of person one should be to be an academic."

In general, an effective mentoring relationship is characterized by mutual respect, trust, understanding, and empathy. Good mentors are able to share life experiences and wisdom, as well as technical expertise. They are *good listeners, good observers,* and *good problem-solvers.* They make an effort to know, accept, and respect the goals and interests of a student. In the end, they establish an environment in which the student's accomplishment is limited only by the extent of his or her talent.

WHY BE A GOOD MENTOR?

The primary motivation to be a mentor was well understood by Homer: the natural human desire to share knowledge and experience. Some other reasons for being a good mentor:

Achieve satisfaction. For some mentors, having a student succeed and eventually become a friend and colleague is their greatest joy.

Attract good students. The best mentors are most likely to be able to recruit—and keep—students of high caliber who can help produce better research, papers, and grant proposals.

Stay on top of your field. There is no better way to keep sharp professionally than to coach junior colleagues.

Develop your professional network. In making contacts for students, you strengthen your own contacts and make new ones.

Extend your contribution. The results of good mentoring live after you, as former students continue to contribute even after you have retired.

FACTS

The Mentoring Relationship

The nature of a mentoring relationship varies with the level and activities of both student and mentor. In general, however, each relationship must be based on a common goal: to advance the educational and personal growth of the student. You as mentor can also benefit enormously.

There is no single formula for good mentoring;

mentoring styles and activities are as varied as human relationships. Different students will require different amounts
and kinds of attention, advice, information, and encouragement. Some students will feel comfortable approaching their
mentors; others will be shy, intimidated, or reluctant to seek
help. A good mentor is approachable and available.

Often students will not know what questions to ask,
what information they need, or what their options are (especially when applying to graduate programs). A good mentor can lessen such confusion by getting to know students
and being familiar with the kinds of suggestions and information that can be useful.

In long-term relationships, friendships form naturally;
students can gradually become colleagues. At the same time,
strive as a mentor to be aware of the distinction between
friendship and favoritism. You might need to remind a student—and yourself—that you need a degree of objectivity
in giving fair grades and evaluations. If you are unsure
whether a relationship is "too personal," you are probably
not alone. Consult with the department chair, your own
mentor, or others you trust. You might have to increase the
mentor-student distance.

Students, for their part, need to understand the professional pressures and time constraints faced by their mentors
and not view them as merely a means—or impediment—to
their goal. For many faculty, mentoring is not their primary
responsibility; in fact, time spent with students can be time
taken from their own research. Students are obliged to recognize the multiple demands on a mentor's time.

At the same time, effective mentoring need not always
require large amounts of time. An experienced, perceptive
mentor can provide great help in just a few minutes by mak-

ing the right suggestion or asking the right question. This section seeks to describe the mentoring relationship by listing several aspects of good mentoring practice.

Careful listening. A good mentor is a good listener. Hear exactly what the student is trying to tell you—without first interpreting or judging. Pay attention to the "subtext" and undertones of the student's words, including tone, attitude, and body language. When you think you have understood a point, it might be helpful to repeat it to the student and ask whether you have understood correctly. Through careful listening, you convey your empathy for the student and your understanding of a student's challenges. When a student feels this empathy, the way is open for clear communication and more-effective mentoring.

Keeping in touch. The amount of attention that a mentor gives will vary widely. A student who is doing well might require only "check-ins" or brief meetings. Another student might have continuing difficulties and require several formal meetings a week; one or two students might occupy most of an adviser's mentoring time. Try through regular contact— daily, if possible—to keep all your students on the "radar screen" to anticipate problems before they become serious. Don't assume that the only students who need help are those who ask for it. Even a student who is doing well could need an occasional, serious conversation. One way to increase your awareness of important student issues and develop rapport is to work with student organizations and initiatives. This will also increase your accessibility to students.

Multiple mentors. No mentor can know everything a given student might need to learn in order to succeed. *Everyone benefits from multiple mentors* of diverse talents, ages, and personalities. No one benefits when a mentor is too "possessive" of a student.

GOOD MENTORING: SEEKING HELP

A white male professor is approached by a black female undergraduate about working in his lab. She is highly motivated, but she worries about academic weaknesses, tells him she is the first member of her family to attend college, and asks for his help. He introduces her to a black male colleague and a white female graduate student in related fields who offer to supplement his advice on course work, planning, and study habits. He also seeks information about fellowships and training programs and forwards this information to the student.

Comment: This student already has an essential quality for academic success—motivation. By taking a few well-planned steps, an alert mentor can help a motivated student initiate a network of contacts, build self-esteem, and fill academic gaps.

STYLES

Sometimes a mentoring team works best. For example, if you are a faculty member advising a physics student who would like to work in the private sector, you might encourage him or her to find mentors in industry as well. A non-Hispanic faculty member advising a Hispanic student might form an advising team that includes a Hispanic faculty member in a related discipline. Other appropriate mentors could include other students, more-advanced postdoctoral associates, and other faculty in the same or other fields. A good place to find additional mentors is in the disciplinary societies, where students can meet scientists, engineers, and students from their own or other institutions at different stages of development.

Coordinate activities with other mentors. For example, a group of mentors might be able to hire an outside speaker or consultant whom you could not afford on your own.

Building networks. You can be a powerful ally for students by helping them build their network of contacts and potential mentors. Advise them to begin with you, other faculty acquaintances, and off-campus people met through jobs, internships, or chapter meetings of professional societies. Building a professional network is a lifelong process that can be crucial in finding a satisfying position and career.

Professional Ethics

Be alert for ways to illustrate ethical issues and choices. The earlier that students are exposed to the notion of scientific integrity, the better prepared they will be to deal with ethical questions that arise in their own work.

Discuss your policies on grades, conflicts of interest, authorship credits, and who goes to meetings. Use real-life questions to help the student understand what is meant by scientific misconduct: What would you do if I asked you to cut corners in your work? What would you do if you had a boss who was unethical?

Most of all, *show by your own example what you mean by ethical conduct.* You might find useful the COSEPUP publication *On Being a Scientist: Responsible Conduct in Research* (1995), also available on line.

Population-Diversity Issues

In years to come, female students and students of minority groups might make up the majority of the population

ADVICE FOR NEW MENTORS

For most people, good mentoring, like good teaching, is a skill that is developed over time. Here are a few tips for beginners:

➤ **Listen patiently.** Give the student time to get to issues they find sensitive or embarrassing.

➤ **Build a relationship.** Simple joint activities—walks across campus, informal conversations over coffee, attending a lecture together—will help to develop rapport. Take cues from the student as to how close they wish this relationship to be. (See "Sexual harassment" in section on Population-diversity issues.)

➤ **Don't abuse your authority.** Don't ask students to do personal work, such as mowing lawns, baby-sitting, and typing.

➤ **Nurture self-sufficiency.** Your goal is not to "clone" yourself but to encourage confidence and independent thinking.

➤ **Establish "protected time" together.** Try to minimize interruptions by telephone calls or visitors.

➤ **Share yourself.** Invite students to see what you do, both on and off the job. Tell of your own successes and failures. Let the student see your human side and encourage the student to reciprocate.

➤ **Provide introductions.** Help the student develop a professional network and build a community of mentors.

➤ **Be constructive.** Critical feedback is essential to spur improvement, but do it kindly and temper criticism with praise when deserved.

➤ **Don't be overbearing.** Avoid dictating choices or controlling a student's behavior.

➤ **Find your own mentors.** New advisers, like new students, benefit from guidance by those with more experience.

TIPS

8

from which scientists and engineers will emerge. Every mentor is challenged to adapt to the growing sex, ethnic, and cultural diversity of both student and faculty populations.

Minority issues. Blacks, Hispanics, and American Indians as a group make up about 23% of the US population, but only about 6% of the science and engineering labor force. Many minority-group students are deterred from careers in science and engineering by inadequate preparation, a scarcity of role models, low expectations on the part of others, and unfamiliarity with the culture and idioms of science. Mentors can often be effective through a style that not only welcomes, nurtures, and encourages questions, but also challenges students to develop critical thinking, self-discipline, and good study habits. Expectations for minority-group students in science have traditionally been too low, and this can have an adverse effect on achievement. A clear statement that you expect the same high performance from all students might prove helpful. Be aware of minority support groups on your campus and of appropriate role models. Link minority-group students with such national support organizations as the National Action Council for Minorities in Engineering (see "Resources").

Cultural issues. You could find yourself advising students of different cultural backgrounds (including those with disabilities) who have different communication and learning styles. Such students might hail from discrete rural or urban cultures in the United States or from abroad; in many programs, foreign-born students are in the majority. If you are not familiar with a particular culture, it is of great importance to demonstrate your willingness to communicate with and to understand each student as a unique individual. Are you baffled by a student's behavior? Remember

POOR MENTORING: CULTURAL BIAS (1)

A foreign-born engineering student is reluctant to question his adviser. As a result, the adviser thinks the student lacks a grasp of engineering. The adviser tries to draw out the student through persistent questioning, which the student finds humiliating. Only the student's determination to succeed prevents him from quitting the program.

Comment: The student grew up in a country where he learned not to question or disagree with a person in authority. Had the adviser suspected that a cultural difference was at the root of the problem, he might have learned quickly why the student was reluctant to question him. When communication is poor, try to share yourself, listen patiently, and ask the students themselves for help.

STYLES

that a cultural difference could be the reason. Don't hesitate to ask colleagues and the students themselves for help. Finding role models is especially important for students from a culture other than yours. Examine yourself for cultural biases or stereotypical thinking.

Female representation. In some fields—notably psychology, the social sciences, and the life sciences—females are well represented as students but underrepresented in the professoriate and are not always appointed to assistant professor positions at a rate that one would expect on the basis of PhD and postdoctoral student representation. In other fields—such as mathematics, physics, computer science, and engineering—females are underrepresented at all levels. In all fields, the confidence of female students might be low, especially where they are isolated and have few female role

POOR MENTORING: CULTURAL BIAS (2)

An American Indian student was having great difficulty in a course, despite genuine effort. A senior professor tutored the student for an entire semester without success. The student failed the course and left for another, less-demanding university. The professor was frustrated at having devoted many hours from his busy schedule and gotten no result.

Comment: Another faculty member decided to seek out the student to see what had happened. The student explained: "In my culture, you would never tell an older person of high authority that you did not understand what he was saying. This would be very disrespectful of his age and wisdom. So I told him I understood, but really I never understood anything he said."

In other words, the student never had told the professor directly that he could not understand him. This information had to be discovered by a third party. If the cultural tradition had been understood, the department might have tried to find a tutor closer to the student's age; the professor could have taken an oversight role to indicate his concern for the student. The student could have been helped, and the professor would have saved time.

STYLES

models. If you advise female students in one of these fields, be aware that they could need extra support. Wait for cues from students, however, to avoid singling out anyone for special treatment. Be familiar with campus support groups and of female role models on and off campus.

Family issues. Both women and men can face challenging family issues; mentors should be alert to students who need extra support when having a child, raising a child alone, returning to school after child-rearing, caring for a

POOR MENTORING: INAPPROPRIATE BEHAVIOR

The male adviser of a female graduate student has not seen her for several months. Passing her in the hall, he squeezes her shoulder as he describes concerns about her research. He sends her an e-mail message, inviting her to discuss the project over dinner. She declines the invitation. He learns that she has redirected her work in a way he does not approve of, and he asks her to return to her original plan. He is astonished when she accuses him of sexual harassment and files a complaint with the dean's office.

Comment: In this case, the adviser erred in touching the student and extending a dinner invitation that could easily be misconstrued.

STYLES

parent, suffering marital problems, or juggling the challenges of a two-career family. You might want to send a student to a colleague or counselor with special competence in family issues.

Sexual harassment. If you mentor a student of the opposite sex, extra sensitivity is required to avoid the appearance of sexual harassment. Inappropriate closeness between mentors and students will produce personal, ethical, and legal consequences not only for the persons involved but also for the programs or institutions of which they are part.

Be guided by common sense and a knowledge of your own circumstances. Is it appropriate to invite the student to discussions at your home? During meetings, should you keep the office door closed (for privacy) or open (to avoid the appearance of intimacy)? Make an effort to forestall mis-understandings by practicing clear communication. If you do have a close friendship with a student, special restrictions or self-imposed behavior changes might be called for.

But do not restrict students' opportunities to interact with you because of sex differences. In a respectful relation-ship, mutual affection can be an appropriate response to shared inquiry and can enhance the learning process; this kind of affection, however, is neither exclusive nor roman-tic. For additional guidance, talk with your department chair, your own mentor, or other faculty.

Disability issues. Students with physical, mental, emo-tional, or learning disabilities constitute about 9% of first-year students with planned majors in science and engineer-ing. Be careful not to underestimate the potential of a student who has a disability. Persons with disabilities who enter the science and engineering workforce perform the same kinds of jobs, in the same fields, as others in the workforce. You should also keep in mind that persons with disabilities might have their own cultural background based on their particular disability, which cuts across ethnic lines.

As a mentor, you might be unsure how to help a student with a disability. Persons with disabilities can function at the same level as other students, but they might need assis-tance to do so. You can play a pivotal role in finding that assistance, assuring students that they are entitled to the assistance, and confirming they are able to secure assistance. Another very important role of the mentor is in making col-leagues comfortable with students who have disabilities.

Many campuses offer programs and aids such as special counseling, special equipment (adaptive computer hard-ware, talking calculators, and communication devices), adapted physical education, learning disability programs, and academic support.

Further, your institution's specialist in Americans with Disabilities Act (ADA) issues might provide help (for example, in securing funding from the National Institutes of Health [NIH], the National Science Foundation [NSF], and other sources). However, keep in mind that this person might know less than you do about the needs of a student in your field—for example, in the use of particular equipment.

Remember that the student who lives with the disability is the expert and that you can ask this expert for help.

WHAT IS A MENTOR?

Summary Points

➤ In a broad sense, a mentor is someone who takes a special interest in helping another develop into a successful professional.

➤ In science and engineering, a good mentor seeks to help a student optimize an educational experience, to assist the student's socialization into a disciplinary culture, and to aid the student in finding suitable employment.

➤ A fundamental difference between a mentor and an adviser is that mentoring is more than advising; mentoring is a personal as well as a professional relationship. An adviser might or might not be a mentor, depending on the quality of the relationship.

➤ An effective mentoring relationship is characterized by mutual trust, understanding, and empathy.

➤ The goal of a mentoring relationship is to advance the educational and personal growth of students.

➤ A good mentor is a good listener.

➤ Everyone benefits from having multiple mentors of diverse talents, ages, and personalities.

➤ A successful mentor is prepared to deal with population-diversity issues, including those peculiar to ethnicity, culture, sex, and disability.

2

THE MENTOR AS FACULTY ADVISER

Faculty advisers can be asked to advise a wide range of students or junior colleagues, from predegree undergraduates to postdoctoral students and junior faculty. The details of your advice will vary widely, but a cardinal goal should be to help those you mentor toward greater initiative, independence, and self-reliance. Those who grow accustomed to nurturing support but who have failed to develop independence might be painfully shocked when moving into a position where such support is lacking. *Students and junior colleagues "own" an important decision only when it is truly theirs.*

Mentoring Undergraduates

When advising undergraduates, you might be asked to help select courses, to suggest work experiences, and to provide guidance as to the many science or engineering careers that are available. Many young students lack sufficient experience to imagine what kind of work they might do as professionals. Don't assume that students know something

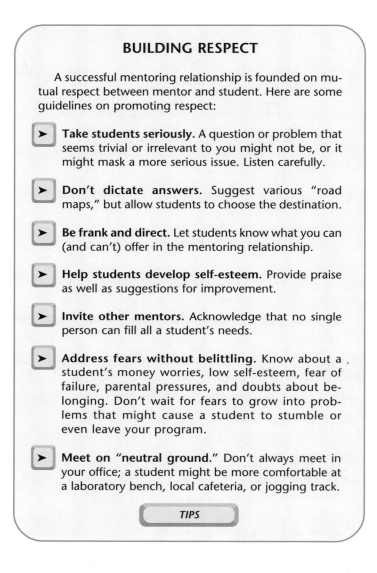

BUILDING RESPECT

A successful mentoring relationship is founded on mutual respect between mentor and student. Here are some guidelines on promoting respect:

➤ **Take students seriously.** A question or problem that seems trivial or irrelevant to you might not be, or it might mask a more serious issue. Listen carefully.

➤ **Don't dictate answers.** Suggest various "road maps," but allow students to choose the destination.

➤ **Be frank and direct.** Let students know what you can (and can't) offer in the mentoring relationship.

➤ **Help students develop self-esteem.** Provide praise as well as suggestions for improvement.

➤ **Invite other mentors.** Acknowledge that no single person can fill all a student's needs.

➤ **Address fears without belittling.** Know about a student's money worries, low self-esteem, fear of failure, parental pressures, and doubts about belonging. Don't wait for fears to grow into problems that might cause a student to stumble or even leave your program.

➤ **Meet on "neutral ground."** Don't always meet in your office; a student might be more comfortable at a laboratory bench, local cafeteria, or jogging track.

TIPS

just because it is obvious to you. One of your goals for students is to provide a "map" to the terrain and a "travelers' guide" to the professional universe that they might some day encounter.

Early concerns. Some students, especially if they are the first in their families to attend college, fear that they lack the ability or preparation to become scientists or engineers. Gently probe the student's level of interest and most-satisfying activities. Introduce a student with low self-confidence to another student or a colleague who faced similar challenges. *Pay special attention to motivation,* which might be more important than background in deciding a student's success or failure. In addition, beware of letting your own assumptions or biases distort your opinion of a student's potential.

An undergraduate might enjoy science and mathematics without knowing how to choose a major. You can help by posing fundamental questions: What have you most enjoyed in life? What are you good at? Do you like abstract problems or hands-on activities? Suggest early exposure to a range of courses, summer jobs or internships, and work-study experiences. Encourage them to explore many options by talking to other students at all levels and to professionals about their careers.

Course work and academic goals. Suppose one of your advisees can't decide whether to major in electrical or chemical engineering. Discussing with students their career goals and discussing the differences between careers might help them decide. In addition, you can suggest colleagues and alumni in those fields, both academic and nonacademic, who would be willing to talk with the student. Suggest that the student undertake an internship or locate a part-time or summer

GOOD MENTORING: ACADEMIC WARNING SIGNS

You are mentor to a hard-working undergraduate whose grades have dropped over the last few months from Bs to Cs. You call him into your office, where you learn that his father has lost his job because of illness and that the student has had to take a part-time job to help the family. You decide with the student that the wisest plan is to reduce his course load for the time being.

Comment: You might have too many undergraduate students for constant, close communication. But by monitoring a few obvious indicators, such as grades, you've been able to detect the symptoms of a problem before it becomes a crisis. This student, by temporarily dropping a course or two, might avoid failures that would mar an otherwise-solid record.

STYLES

job. The National Science Foundation's Research Experiences for Undergraduates Program offers both summer and in-term paid research experiences. Your institution's research-support office, placement office, or alumni association might be good resources, as are national disciplinary societies and your own personal contacts.

For electives, encourage students to take courses that they enjoy or that can lead to new fields of study. The undergraduate years offer the opportunity for experimentation with fields of knowledge. As their career unfolds, they might work outside their field, outside research, or outside their native country; courses in business, psychology, public policy, or foreign language might open new doors; courses in arts and humanities will provide breadth and perspective. A biology major interested in genetics might take a class in psychology and find an interest in genetic counseling. A physics major who is exposed to health care might discover a career in radiation physics. On the other hand, students also should learn the importance of focus and depth in some field.

Urge the student to seek practical experience. Eventual hiring decisions are often influenced more by students' accumulated laboratory experiences, computer skills, or industrial training than by the courses they have taken. A reference from someone who has worked with the student in a practical context carries additional weight. A volunteer summer position with a good teacher or laboratory might be worth more than a summer job that pays well but teaches little, even if this involves short-term financial sacrifice.

Undergraduate research. Encourage undergraduate students to perform a research project, whether with you or a colleague, so that they better understand the practice of science. This experience is valuable regardless of the career path chosen. If you are the research adviser, help the student find a well-planned project that interests both of you and that can be completed in a defined period.

Work with the student to set up a clear time line for completion of research. Set high but realistic goals; it is very important to select a project that has a good chance of success. Define your own responsibilities, including regular feedback and evaluation. Make connections between course work and the literature.

For the committed student, such a project can have lasting influence, whether the student goes on to graduate school or directly into the workforce. Do *not*, however, place undergraduates in research posts without evaluating their fitness and desire to perform the work. And do not assign undergraduates to a pilot program or an untested method.

POOR MENTORING: WHEN IS A RISK WORTH TAKING?

An undergraduate biology major tells his adviser that he wants to do an ambitious summer research project. The adviser explains that the project will require knowledge of molecular genetics and microbiology, which the student has not yet studied. In addition, the student would have no supervision. But the student is adamant, and she relents.

Comment: The mentor is aware of the potential value of a challenging project; learning what one needs to know is a life skill. And she wants to show respect for the student by honoring his judgment. But in this instance she might be allowing him to begin a project that will yield only frustration. Research that is poorly conceived or unsupervised can even detract from a student's educational experience.

STYLES

Research that is poorly conceptualized or executed might be worse than no research experience at all. If a student does have a poor research experience, try to explain the reasons; a student who understands the causes of failure is less likely to suffer permanent career damage.

Your broader challenge is to interpret a research experience in the context of the student's total education. The primary purposes of student research are to master techniques, to learn to think critically, to acquire strategies for problem-solving, and to learn the importance of patience and perseverance in the unpredictable context of research.

An excellent source of information and support is the Council on Undergraduate Research (CUR), a national organization founded on the premise that research adds depth and problem-solving ability to the learning of science. CUR, based at the University of North Carolina in Asheville, supports publications, workshops, formal meetings, consulting services, speaking programs, fellowships, and a home page (see "Internet Resources").

Another resource is Project Kaleidoscope (PKAL), an informal national alliance that seeks to strengthen undergraduate programs in science, mathematics, engineering, and technology. The vision of PKAL is to promote "a thriving community of students and faculty working together in a research-rich environment." The organization, headquartered in Washington, DC, sponsors workshops, seminars, consulting teams, and Internet links (see "Internet Resources").

Contemplating graduate school. How can you tell whether a student has what it takes for graduate school? The usual indicators are references, course records, test scores, and success in undergraduate research. But don't be afraid to use your intuition: Do you detect the energy of curiosity and motivation? *The truly motivated student will probably find a way to succeed.*

On the other hand, the rigorous environment of graduate school is not a good place for hesitant students to avoid the "real world" or to pass time while deciding what to do with their lives. Graduate study requires high levels of commitment and ability.

Mentoring Graduate Students

Many science-related careers do not require a PhD. In such fields as biotechnology, hydrogeology, environmental engineering, science and technology policy analysis, and science

23

journalism, the bachelor's or master's degree can lead directly to a productive career. It is common for engineers to terminate their studies at the bachelor's or master's level; some engineers add a master's degree after beginning employment.

A doctorate is appropriate for most students who desire research careers, including academic research and industrial research. But a doctorate does not restrict a person to a life at the bench or in academe. For example, of senior scientists and engineers employed in business or industry, one-third are in management.

Choosing a school. If students are ready to make the leap to graduate school, encourage them to use the telephone, visit campuses (and their home pages), talk with current students and faculty, seek out alumni, attend conferences, and read publications by faculty. Personal meetings with professionals and students can bring a feel for the profession and an excellent basis for choosing an appropriate learning environment.

Helping students choose an adviser. At the graduate level, *students' choice of a research adviser is one of their most important decisions*—and yet some of them exercise less care in this decision than they do in the purchase of a car. Encourage students to shop around carefully, to talk to present and former advisees, and to gain personal impressions through face-to-face interviews. Be sure that a potential student knows your particular mentoring style and finds it congenial.

Students should also be advised to examine the performance of possible mentors: publication record, financial-support base, reputation, success of recent graduates, recognition of student accomplishments (e.g., through coauthorship),

A Mathematics Major
Who Became an Actuary

Russell Greig excelled in mathematics as an undergraduate at Florida A&M University. His goals were to use mathematics in a practical way, to work in the "real world," and to earn a good income. He was planning a career in civil engineering when his calculus professor took him aside.

"He said, 'You're doing well enough in math; have you considered actuarial science?' I hadn't, so I checked it out in the *Jobs Almanac*, which said it was a growing field. After some reluctance—I was already pretty far along in engineering—I decided to give it a try.'"

Now, just 5 years later, Mr. Greig is one examination away from being a fellow of the Casualty Actuarial Society, the rough equivalent of a PhD in actuarial mathematics. He gained a head start by taking the first two actuarial examinations as an undergraduate; 10 are required for fellowship status. As a result, he was offered a job by the National Council on Compensation Insurance, in Boca Raton, FL, an insurance advisory company. His first assignment was to produce new data on workers' compensation claims needed by insurance companies, actuaries, and legislatures. He is now calculating reserves for the workers' compensation "residual" insurance market. At the same time, he is approaching the end of his studies.

"Since I graduated, I've been spending close to 400 hours every 4 months studying for the exams," he says.

continued

PROFILE

"The company gives me 120 hours, the rest I do at night and on weekends. The competition is pretty steep, so you have to do well. If you do, job prospects are excellent and you gain high respect in the profession. At the fellowship level you're at the top and you can pretty much decide where you want to work. I'll probably stay in the South; I'm from the Virgin Islands and I can't take the cold."

Mr. Greig encourages students who enjoy applied mathematics to look into the field. "I recommend it to those who enjoy number-crunching, who want to see immediate, practical results from what they're doing. You have to be prepared to pay your dues, but there's plenty of opportunity. There are only about 2,500 casualty actuaries in the world, and the field is still growing.

"Math majors have other good choices in applied fields. One is the financial area, where there is demand for people who can quantify financial-risk models and can present clearly what they're doing to others who are not sophisticated in math. In fact, when I'm done with these exams I'm going to take the Chartered Financial Analyst exams, which are like a shortcut to an MBA in finance. This allows you to do more asset-related work.

"Another growth area is computer science and programming. I often work with programmers who don't understand the math involved. If you know the math to begin with, you'll be able to write your own ticket. The math is where it begins."

PROFILE

laboratory organization, and, most important, willingness to spend time with students. Much of this information can be learned directly from the potential mentor and from the mentor's current and past students.

Which students should you accept? You might be approached by more than one student about being an adviser. Bear in mind the responsibilities of saying yes, and examine your other commitments. Handling a large group might be possible with a "secondary mentoring" network, where senior members of your research group act as mentors to junior members.

Remind yourself, and students whom you consider taking on, of the importance of personal chemistry. Do you think you can work productively with this person? Can you imagine recommending this student for a job? If the relationship doesn't feel right for either party, or if communication is poor, think about helping the student find another adviser as soon as possible. You might also consider developing the skills that will allow you to work with a more-diverse group of students.

Choosing a degree program. Many students on the threshold of graduate school are unable to visualize a career path; this makes it difficult to choose a degree program. Remind them that *careers evolve slowly*, and ask the kinds of basic questions you would ask an undergraduate: What are you good at? What kinds of activities are most satisfying? How much schooling do you need to do that?

Keep in mind that science and engineering degrees can often be combined in interesting ways with such professional degrees as the MBA, JD, and MD. For example, a student might combine degrees in microbiology and law for a career in patent law. A physics major might add a minor in business, or even Japanese studies, with an eye to a position with a multinational corporation.

The decision to pursue a doctorate might entail some sacrifice. Student A, who moves directly into the job market after a bachelor's or master's degree, might be well ahead in experience and financial gain by the time Student B receives a PhD. Over the course of a career, Student B might reach higher levels of salary and responsibility, but not for some time.

Planning the curriculum. When a new graduate student arrives at your institution, discuss the rules regarding required and elective courses, comprehensive exams, thesis, and teaching. Requirements vary even within an institution. Keep handy your institution's student handbook or course guide for continuing discussions.

Some programs, such as environmental studies and earth sciences, might naturally encompass a wide range of topics. Others are more sharply focused in subject matter, and leave less room for exploration. Where appropriate, encourage students to *seek classes that will expand their knowledge base* and help develop requirements for such classes. Some students benefit from auditing nontechnical classes, such as business and law, or taking classes in another university through a consortium program ("Course work and academic goals" in the above section on "Mentoring Undergraduates"). In all cases, students should first talk with the instructor and with students who have taken the course to assess whether it will meet their needs.

When planning their curriculum, graduate students at all levels should be aware of nonacademic and interdisciplinary career opportunities. As noted in the "Logistical Issues" box, most recent science and engineering PhDs are not

28

GOOD MENTORING: SOCIALIZATION

You have a dozen graduate students in your busy laboratory. Most are doing well, but two are introverted and have little awareness of what goes on outside. You have no time for extensive briefings; instead, you suggest that they accompany you to a professional meeting. You also suggest they each write a proposal for travel funds. You travel with them, find opportunities to chat, and introduce them to colleagues at the meeting.

Comment: With a small investment of time, you have shown these students that a career in science is more than laboratory work. You have offered a glimpse of your professional world, helped them initiate their own network of colleagues, and suggested the importance of good "people skills." And by encouraging them to raise their own travel funds, you have shown them how to take an initiative in broadening their professional horizons.

STYLES

---

employed in traditional academic positions. Many disciplinary societies profile people with advanced degrees in their publications and Web pages, many of whom have found satisfying alternative careers. An extended discussion of this issue, including a series of profiles, is offered in the COSEPUP publication *Careers in Science and Engineering: A Student Planning Guide to Grad School and Beyond* (see "Resources"). A few of these profiles are included in this guide.

Choosing a research topic. Urge the student to think through a research topic in advance—to imagine a thesis title, list hypotheses to test and perhaps expected outcomes, and write a full proposal. The title and outcomes might

THREE LOGISTICAL ISSUES TO DISCUSS WITH DOCTORAL AND POSTDOCTORAL CANDIDATES

If you mentor students who aspire to doctoral degrees, it is your responsibility to make sure that they know several key facts. Students who attain doctorates and seek to enter the job market without knowing these facts might feel, with some justification, betrayed by their mentors.

Employment

➤ Fewer than 50% of those with doctoral science degrees are employed in academe—a proportion that has been decreasing since the early 1970s. Only one-third are in tenure-track positions.

➤ It has long been true in engineering that about one-third of PhDs find positions in academe. The experience in engineering might be the model of the future for all fields of science and engineering.

➤ The number of doctoral scientists and engineers employed in industry and business has been increasing steadily. Federal employment has been constant while other categories of employment have been increasing slowly.

➤ Unemployment rates for recent doctoral science and engineering graduates in some fields have at times been greater than 10%. To understand the employment situation for their particular fields, students should obtain information from their disciplinary societies.

➤ Doctoral scientists and engineers are taking longer to locate employment. Students should not limit their employment search to academe; if they do not succeed, they will only have delayed the possibility of employment in business, industry, or elsewhere.

FACTS

Time to Degree

➤ The median number of years between receipt of the bachelor's degree and the doctorate in science or engineering for 1995 was about 9 years (see figure).

MEDIAN TIME TO DEGREE
FROM BACCALAUREATE TO DOCTORATE (1995)

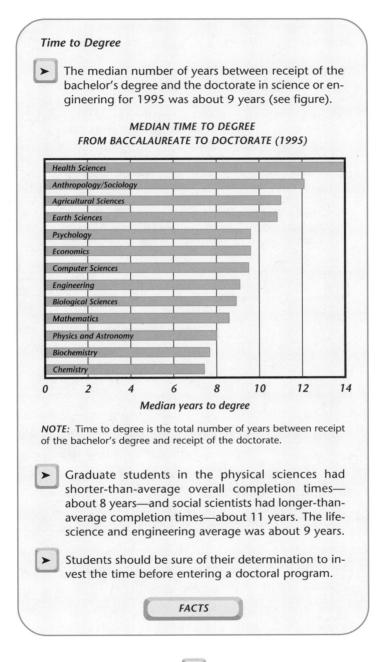

Median years to degree

NOTE: Time to degree is the total number of years between receipt of the bachelor's degree and receipt of the doctorate.

➤ Graduate students in the physical sciences had shorter-than-average overall completion times—about 8 years—and social scientists had longer-than-average completion times—about 11 years. The life-science and engineering average was about 9 years.

➤ Students should be sure of their determination to invest the time before entering a doctoral program.

FACTS

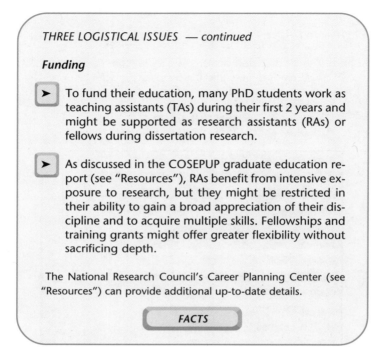

THREE LOGISTICAL ISSUES — *continued*

Funding

➤ To fund their education, many PhD students work as teaching assistants (TAs) during their first 2 years and might be supported as research assistants (RAs) or fellows during dissertation research.

➤ As discussed in the COSEPUP graduate education report (see "Resources"), RAs benefit from intensive exposure to research, but they might be restricted in their ability to gain a broad appreciation of their discipline and to acquire multiple skills. Fellowships and training grants might offer greater flexibility without sacrificing depth.

The National Research Council's Career Planning Center (see "Resources") can provide additional up-to-date details.

FACTS

change, but a well-designed planning procedure (perhaps including a public presentation and defense) helps both you and the student toward a common understanding of the project. It also allows other committee members to contribute early in the process. If you approve a topic outside your expertise, recruit a committee member who is an expert.

Discuss with the student whether the project meets these conditions; it should interest you as well as the student, permit the student to learn useful skills, serve as the basis for a thesis no matter what the results, and be designed for completion within a reasonable period. Students who are part of a large group should be able to claim a particular aspect of the work that can be developed further.

Choosing a committee. Both mentor and student should participate in choosing a committee. Be sure the group represents a good mix of ages, fields, analytic approaches, and other qualities. If you as research adviser have a practical bent, a colleague who is a theorist might add good balance. Share with the student any knowledge of personal or political conflicts among potential members, which could disrupt a student's progress and morale.

Some students are tempted to seek members who are unlikely to be critical. You should encourage students to avoid this strategy. The members of a committee should be respected as scholars and have the expertise needed to give thorough exams and supervise research. The student needs committee members who will form the nucleus of a professional network and eventually help the student find employment and a satisfying career path.

Making good progress. Part of the mentor's job is to *teach careful planning and use of time.* Let students know what their responsibilities are and agree on schedules. If a student falls behind, consider that the cause might be exhaustion, unclear direction, lack of commitment, or dislike for the project or persons involved. Suggest breaking a large task into smaller pieces, "easing" into it by steps, and setting a time limit for each step. Encourage the student to set aside regular time for planning and also for self-improvement (reflective thought, physical exercise, reading for pleasure, and so on).

Students benefit from writing regular progress reports (preferably in the form of research articles) to clarify their own work, to communicate with you, and to sharpen their writing skills. You might choose to have weekly research-group meetings where students take turns presenting papers and exchanging experiences. Make presentations informal, with time for many questions.

Powerful forces can work against making good progress. You or other faculty might seek to retain students as they become more proficient. That is an unfortunate conflict between your desire to maximize productivity in your own research and your duty as a mentor to support a student's timely progress. *Your primary obligation is to the education of the student.*

Students, too, can be reluctant to conclude their research, either because they have not found employment or because they don't know what to do next. Urge them to push against those forces. The students' goal should be to finish in a timely fashion, and this should be your goal for them as well.

At the same time, discourage rigid schedules. Remember that every student is unique, and many end up doing things differently—and often much better—than you might have imagined. Some students, through no fault of their own, will require extra time: new parents (fathers as well as mothers), those who work part time, students with disabilities, those who return after an off-campus fellowship or other leave of absence, and so on.

If, after a reasonable period, a student has not shown high aptitude for research, the mentor should advise a nonresearch career. This can be difficult if a student has planned a research career, but if you are convinced that a student's abilities are insufficient or are stronger in another field, the kindest course is to say so.

Abuse of power. Many students, especially in graduate school, are profoundly dependent on their mentors—often for a combination of financial, educational, and emotional support. *This dependence makes it easy for advisers to abuse their power* (sometimes unintentionally) and difficult for students to contest an abuse. Advisers might give inadequate credit for students' research or assign work of little or no educational value. They might impair a student's confidence by too much criticism, too little support, or emotional indifference.

Abuses of power can be especially hard to resolve when the person best positioned to help solve the problem is central to the problem. It is best to discuss such issues face to face; when appropriate, committee members, other faculty, or a department chair can mediate. If a colleague or student has raised an abuse-of-power issue with you, consult with other mentors, strive for better communication with students, or ask for help from a third party.

Professional growth. There are many ways to facilitate students' professional growth in addition to one-on-one counseling. One strategy is to create informal cross-disciplinary groups (such as women in mathematics and science). Use monthly meetings (with incentives like free pizza) as forums for discussing such topics as interview strategies, coping with negative reviews, and giving good presentations. Another approach is to organize interdisciplinary seminars with other departments to introduce students (and faculty) to new avenues of inquiry and to colleagues in related disciplines.

Make use of your network of contacts to suggest internships, summer or part-time jobs, and off-campus mentoring. Propose an active role in student chapters of professional societies, where students can gain group skills, learn about career possibilities, and make valuable contacts among both peers and professors. Other suggestions are presented in the section "Mentoring Undergraduates."

Mentoring Postdoctoral Students

Postdoctoral study has become the norm in some fields, such as the life sciences and chemical sciences; for other fields, such as engineering, it is rare. Some students find that a postdoctoral study in a national or industrial laboratory broadens their outlook and job opportunities and allows them to learn a new research culture. Others find themselves in a "holding pattern"—going from postdoctoral position to postdoctoral position without finding a long-term research position—as well as working for low pay and no benefits for many years. Thus, the decision to undertake postdoctoral work should not be made lightly and should be made only after examination of one's career goals and the career opportunities in that field.

Finding a position. Encourage students who want a postdoctoral position to determine the three or four research groups that seem most appropriate to their interests and abilities. Use your own network of contacts and make personal calls to introduce the student. Then suggest that the student call each supervisor, with relevant questions: How many postdoctoral fellows do you have now? What do they do? Where do they go afterward? What support is available? Recommend a face-to-face meeting with the supervisor, as well as with former postdoctoral students of the program and faculty members doing similar work.

The need for postdoctoral mentoring. It can be tempting to suppose that postdoctoral students require little or no mentoring because they have more experience than undergraduate or graduate students. That might not be true for postdoctoral students, any more than it is for junior faculty.

A RESUME OR A CV?

Most job-seekers need to provide potential employers with a written record of who they are and what they have done. If you are asked for advice, remember that there are as many ways to do this as there are job-seekers—and employers. Here are a few pointers:

A CV is the traditional "long form" used in applying for an academic position. It includes all published works, presentations, awards, and educational history.

A resume is a more-concise presentation whose content varies with one's particular history and the kind of position sought. Categories of resumes are:

➤ A chronologic resume, which simply documents work experience and education in chronological order.

➤ A functional or targeted resume, which focuses on specific abilities and achievements, listed in order as they are related to a specific field or position being sought.

For more specific guidance, see "Resources."

FACTS

In fact, postdoctoral students, who might have scant supervision, ill-defined goals, and poor access to a community of peers—tend to incur greater risks of isolation and stagnation than graduate students. A good mentoring relationship can be crucial to the success of postdoctoral students as they develop original research ideas and move toward greater independence and maturity.

Helping the student find a second or even third postdoctoral position might not be difficult, but the most-valuable contribution of the mentor is to help the student find a "real job." That process should occur before the student begins their research with a thorough review of the student's experience and goals. Establish your expectations and "terms of employment." Set a schedule for follow-up reviews at regular intervals. Career goals, which can change appreciably over time, should be a central topic of these discussions. Another important topic is finances; postdoctoral students often enter a postdoctoral position with scant financial resources. Be aware of ethical employment practices, which include giving advance notice of layoffs and regular updates on a postdoctoral student's employment status.

Some of the basic obligations that a mentor has to a postdoctoral student are to help perform research, design a good curriculum vitae, rehearse interviews, prepare manuscripts, plan seminars, raise grant money, and learn about the current job market (see the box "Career Questions"). In addition, a good mentor will maintain sufficiently frequent contact to know about personal or other problems that could hinder progress and will generally make every necessary effort to help the postdoctoral student grow into a mature and productive colleague.

Demonstrating progress. In any field, the broad purpose of the postdoctoral experience is to gain research experience and skills that open new vistas. If you mentor postdoctoral students, make it clear that they should demonstrate independent research thinking, be productive, have their work reflected on their record, and make sure that someone in a position of authority knows what they are doing and can facilitate their next steps.

Some students find it useful to remain with a laboratory after the usual 1-3 years of postdoctoral experience. However, this should be accompanied by clear indications of progress, such as promotion to research associate (or other position), the addition of responsibilities (such as supervision and teaching), and efforts to obtain independent funding.

A common problem of postdoctoral students is their lack of institutional connections. Mentors can help by making them aware of the nature and location of department offices and by introducing them to other faculty and staff—an obvious step that is often ignored. Encourage the department or institution to include postdoctoral students in their seminars, retreats, and meetings with speakers.

Further comments of relevance to postdoctoral students are offered in the next section, on mentoring junior faculty.

Mentoring Junior Faculty

When a department hires a new assistant professor, it has invested one of its most valuable resources: a tenure-track position. And yet new faculty are often left to fend for themselves amid the turmoil of professional and personal change: new courses to teach, a laboratory empty of both equipment and students, unknown department politics, conflicting demands on one's time, an unfamiliar living environment.

As a result, it is not surprising that faculty retreats and discussions at a number of universities have revealed extensive morale problems among junior faculty, including a sense of isolation and alienation. Those expressing dissatisfaction are not restricted to females and minority-group faculty, who might have few or no role models among senior faculty, but include white males as well.

Although research on this subject is sorely needed, an effective way to increase the likelihood of retaining talented young faculty might be to provide excellent guidance by senior mentors. Even through relatively simple mechanisms, such as luncheons and workshops with senior faculty, junior faculty can obtain needed guidance on career goals, ethical behavior, housing and financial issues, collaborative relationships, grant-proposal writing, resource people, teaching policies, department politics, personal issues, and criteria for appointments, promotions, tenure, and salary.

Some institutions (for example, Stanford) have initiated mentoring programs that match each new faculty member with a senior mentor. The mentors are encouraged to offer advice, guidance, and, when necessary, intervention with administration or other faculty on behalf of their junior partners. Mentoring pairs might meet at least several times a year to discuss such topics as career options, space allocation, funding, and research. Sometimes a written mentoring agreement is useful in formalizing the expectations of both parties.

Both senior faculty and the department chair can play important roles in setting the tone and agenda for mentoring junior faculty. Be aware that junior faculty members might not have had useful mentoring themselves and so might need extra guidance in helping their own students. In particular, the chair and other leaders should

➤ Make clear the expectations and criteria for promotion. Be sure that the new faculty members understand timetables and deadlines, what is required for tenure, and exactly how new faculty are evaluated.

➤ Facilitate the acquisition of resources to meet those expectations. Introduce new faculty to the rest of the faculty and to key staff people. Facilitate research by securing a good startup package; send promising graduate students their way. Give new faculty a list of teaching policies and help, if needed, in learning to teach well.

➤ Give frequent, accurate feedback. Formally evaluate junior faculty at least once a year—preferably twice. Appoint an ad hoc review committee to meet with the new faculty member. At the meeting, ask about short-term and long-term goals. Discuss the committee's report at a meeting of tenured faculty, and then discuss the evaluations with the new faculty member.

➤ Reduce impediments to progress toward promotion. Protect women and minority-group faculty from the demands of "tokenism" when many people will assume that women and minority-group faculty are the only ones who can advise women or minority-group students. Protect new faculty from excessive requests from senior faculty, and from exploitation in group grants or facilities. Facilitate access to nonacademic resources (such as medical care, child care, and housing) and be aware of family and dual-career issues.

Summary Points

➤ **Undergraduates:** One of your goals should be to assist inexperienced students to gain a "feel" for the many different careers in science and engineering. Early exposure to a range of courses, summer jobs or internships, and work-study experiences can help students find the right major and envision subsequent goals. Performing a well-planned research project can help them understand the practice of science and add value to their education regardless of the career path they choose.

➤ **Graduate students:** The career advice for undergraduate mentoring is true for graduate students as well. Although a graduate student might make important contributions to your own research program, the primary obligation of the mentor is to further the student's education. One goal for students should be to finish their degree program in a timely fashion, and this should be your goal for them as well.

➤ **Postdoctoral students:** Postdoctoral students, who might have a weak relationship with the institution where they work, often receive inadequate guidance. Mentors can make crucial contributions to a postdoctoral student's career in helping to focus goals and to find the next position.

➤ **Junior faculty:** New professors, who commonly suffer from the pressures of conflicting demands and overlapping challenges, need mentoring as much as new students do. Some institutions have benefited by pairing new faculty with senior professors, who can provide invaluable guidance and feedback.

THE MENTOR AS
CAREER ADVISER

Good mentoring in science and engineering has taken on added importance in recent years. Over the last 2 decades, the proportion of PhDs entering traditional academic research and teaching has dropped from over 60% to less than 50%; thus, most new PhDs today find work outside academe. Most scientists and engineers are entering a more diverse employment environment that is characterized by a trend toward more-interdisciplinary, collaborative, and team work. Many of them are preparing for more-integrative, systemic approaches to increasingly complex fields, such as bioscience, environmental studies, and information science.

As the employment environment and the conduct of science and engineering change continuously, *it is wise to view the career as an evolutionary process.* Students should plan their careers with an eye to steady or even sudden change. They might not know exactly how they will use their education until they begin professional work.

One of the most helpful things you can do for students

APTITUDES AND GOALS

Students are not always aware of all their talents; this makes it hard for them to envision a career. Encourage them early to make an inventory of their aptitudes and to weigh these in the context of various goals. Counseling centers can offer psychologic tests or self-assessment exercises. Career planning centers might suggest books, computer programs, and other tools. Urge them to meet people in the fields that they contemplate entering.

TIPS

at any stage is to take them on visits to other laboratories or to industrial work sites. Such visits can give students a broad and realistic view of possible careers.

Envisioning and Planning a Career

Even though students cannot know which direction their careers will eventually take, they can help themselves by studying the possibilities. One of the mentor's goals should be to help the student stay aware of evolving career conditions and opportunities.

Encourage students to find out what recent graduates from their department or program have done. Help them recognize fields that are likely to be expanding when they graduate. Many "hot" fields involve cross-disciplinary research and therefore a combination of educational backgrounds and skills. Be aware, however, that a popular field might attract more students than there are jobs.

In preparing for a career, advise a balance between

TWO KEY CAREER QUESTIONS TO DISCUSS WITH STUDENTS

Many students have little understanding of how their education can lead to a career in science or engineering. As a mentor, one of your greatest contributions can be to help them ask the right kinds of questions well in advance of important career decisions.

➤ **What kind of job can I expect?** Students at all levels should understand that they will face a challenging and ever-changing job situation; finding employment in science or engineering is hard work. They need to be prepared for a variety of careers no matter what their degree level. Even at the PhD level, securing a satisfying position takes planning, networking, and, often, luck. It is important that mentors encourage students to actively seek out a variety of occupations—particularly those in new niches in growing sectors of the economy—and to gain experiences through internships or summer employment.

If students ask you what can be done with a degree in a particular field, encourage them to visit the Catapult Web site, run by the National Association of Colleges and Employers (http://www.jobweb.org/catapult/choice.htm). Catapult provides lists of resources and tools that allow students to evaluate their aptitude for various occupations. Your on-site career planning center might have resources as well.

➤ **What kind of career can I expect?** Many students envision a career path that begins with the undergraduate degree and leads in a straight line to an imagined goal. In real life, most careers move through a series of branching decision points. The development of multiple abilities, including practical experiences and communication skills, can allow students to take best advantage of these decision points.

continued

TIPS

45

TWO KEY CAREER QUESTIONS — continued

For example, some students benefit from working for a year or so, rather than moving straight into graduate school. That can allow them to decide better what the next step in their career should be. Their employer might even be willing to foot the bill for graduate study, whether in science or engineering or in business, law, or medicine.

You might wish to encourage your students to read the COSEPUP guide *Careers in Science and Engineering: A Student Planning Guide to Grad School and Beyond,* which discusses these issues at greater length (see "Resources"). The full text is available on line (http://www.nap.edureadingroom/books/careers) at no charge.

TIPS

breadth and specialization. A major in a very broad area might not provide the specific skills needed to land a job. Conversely, over specialization can be perilous; today's hot technology could be outmoded in 5 years. An engineer with a narrow base of education, such as an exclusive focus on aeronautical engineering, might be more vulnerable to job-market changes than one with a more-general degree, such as mechanical or electrical engineering.

Undergraduates: Early Perspectives

Many undergraduates have little idea what kind of career they can anticipate. If you as mentor are happy and successful in what you do, it might be natural to encourage a student to follow in your footsteps. Remember, however, that each student is unique and needs to be encouraged to select the most-appropriate path for him or her. Avoid the

WRITING LETTERS OF RECOMMENDATION

Mentors are often asked to write formal letters on behalf of present or former students. The task can be simplified by keeping a notebook on specific student activities and achievements. A half-dozen brief entries can enable you to write a useful letter when the time comes.
Some tips on content:

➤ **Be honest with students.** If you cannot write a supportive letter, tell the student beforehand. It is only fair to indicate the level of praise that the student can expect.

➤ **Be honest with readers.** Identify whether information comes from personal knowledge or second-hand sources, such as institutional files. Indicate whether the letter is confidential or open for review by the student.

➤ **Be specific.** Can you describe a student's excellent laboratory report, keen insight, or team skill? Such details bring the student to life. Be quantitative, when possible, describing a student's positive characteristics: e.g., "among the postdoctoral students I have had, this applicant ranks in the ___ percentile in terms of research potential, teaching ability, etc."

➤ **Be relevant.** Describe qualities or achievements related to the position under consideration.

➤ **Get your facts straight,** especially about former students. Is that the Jane Smith who went into radiology or radio astronomy? Remind former students to send you a current CV and a description of the desired position so that your letter can be focused and up to date.

➤ **Share your insights.** Although it is seldom possible to predict how a given student will turn out, this does not mean that you have nothing to say. Your honest insight might be just what an admissions officer or potential employer needs to make a decision.

➤ **Keep copies of previous** letters to serve as starting points.

TIPS

GOOD MENTORING: BEING FLEXIBLE

A first-generation university student compiles a good record in his engineering major and in undergraduate research. His mentor strongly encourages him to pursue graduate study in the mentor's field, but the student feels an obligation to repay debts that he has accumulated and does not feel ready for graduate school. The mentor finds funds to send him to a national meeting where he makes contacts that lead to an industrial job in his field. After 3 years, he applies to graduate school and is able to choose from among several programs.

Comment: Students follow many paths to reach their goals. Mentors should be careful not to insist that students follow their mentors' suggested career pathways.

STYLES

temptation to treat students as "clones" of yourself (see box "Good Mentoring: Being Flexible").

One challenge for many mentors is to stay current on employment trends in their field, especially if they have worked on campus for many years. You can monitor major trends with a small investment of time by visiting some of the on line sites mentioned in "Resources." And you can investigate the local career-planning center and your institution's alumni network. Encourage students to visit workplaces, to arrange to "shadow" people on the job, and to find off-campus internships and summer placements. *There is no substitute for practical experience* in learning what one is good at, what a field is like, and what scientists and engineers actually do.

When a student has trouble articulating goals, be patient. As long as students are interested and engaged in their work, they shouldn't be pressured. *Goals must evolve at a natural pace.* Remind students that they will almost certainly have multiple positions and perhaps even multiple careers, which is the strongest reason to aim for flexibility in qualification and experience.

Graduate Students:
Helping Students Become Colleagues

Once a student begins a job search in earnest, there are many ways the mentor can help, from encouragement and advice to direct recommendations. When possible, arrange a telephone call or face-to-face meeting, which can be far more persuasive than a letter. *Introduce students to members of your own network* of contacts and urge them to extend that network themselves.

Recommend other search aids, including Internet sources (such as the NRC Career Planning Center), professional societies, and ads in journals and major newspapers. Keep handy your own list of telephone numbers and addresses, especially of former students, that might be helpful. (See "Resources" for more ideas.)

After spending years in graduate school, some students might devalue their own abilities or feel that they are too specialized for many employment positions. Remind them that they have acquired not only a series of credentials and a vocation, but a range of transferable skills—including analytical reasoning, program design and management, communication, evaluation, integration, and objectivity—that can be applied in many occupations.

POOR MENTORING: HONEST ADVICE

You are the thesis adviser for a PhD student whose heart is set on a tenure-track research position at a major university. You feel strongly that the student lacks the abilities for such a position, but you do not tell the student, and your letters of recommendation are luke-warm. The student is angry and confused when numerous applications are turned down.

Comment: Part of the mentor's job is to help the student find satisfying employment. That is difficult or impossible when the student's goals are not well aligned with abilities. You can best serve the student's interest by discussing this issue frankly and, when appropriate, suggesting alternative goals (a career in developmental research or teaching, for example) that might bring more satisfaction.

At the same time, be alert for biased assumptions on your part (e.g., "women are best at teaching" or "he lacks the intuitive instinct of a real researcher"). You might not know all there is to know about a student's abilities or goals; the best you can offer is your own honest, but sometimes limited, perspective.

STYLES

Postdoctoral Students: Finding a "Real" Job

Mentors can help postdoctoral students prepare for jobs by helping them to sharpen the skills listed above and to design a good CV, rehearse interviews, and learn about the current job market. In many cases, the most useful function of mentors is to introduce postdoctoral student to their own contacts, who might be able to offer or point to desirable positions.

Help students be aware of local resources for job-seekers, including the institution's career center, bulletin boards, or professional meetings where jobs are advertised.

Keep in touch with candidates' progress by discussing the results of their interviews and job applications. Many faculty avoid this subject and end up offering insensitive or irrelevant advice.

Discuss career goals with the postdoctoral students and provide honest feedback, even when this is difficult. Provide examples of nonacademic, as well as academic, role models.

The Career as Continuum

At every level, the student should learn to look at academic and professional activities as parts of a single or branching continuum. As the student views course work, summer jobs, and practical experience as part of a single journey, the transition from student to professional activities can be smooth and satisfying. Each student activity is best regarded as a long-term investment in a life's work.

Summary Points

 Advise students that a career is seldom a straight line to an imagined goal. Careers today are usually a series of "branching decision points" requiring an increasing degree of flexibility and versatility.

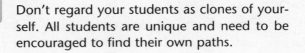 Suggest a balance between breadth and specialization. Too much breadth might not provide needed expertise; overspecialization can be perilous if a "hot" field or technique suddenly cools.

 Don't regard your students as clones of yourself. All students are unique and need to be encouraged to find their own paths.

 Encourage off-campus internships and part-time or temporary jobs. There is no substitute for practical experience in the workplace.

 Introduce students to members of your own professional network.

Be aware of local resources for job-seekers, including your institution's career center, bulletin boards, Internet sites (see "Resources"), and professional meetings where jobs are advertised.

Keep in touch with job-seekers' progress by discussing results of their interviews and job applications. Be a partner in the job search.

4

THE MENTOR AS SKILLS CONSULTANT

Students must augment their field-specific knowledge and experience with a variety of other skills if they are to make the best use of their talents. Beyond learning to communicate about science, many students need to develop informal communication skills in general, such as the ability to express themselves clearly and understand others' responses. You can help them develop these other skills in the context of many learning activities.

Developing Skills as an Undergraduate

Planning and organization. Many undergraduates have little experience in organizing tasks and making good use of time. You can help them acquire this skill, beginning with simple scheduling. Use mentoring appointments as a framework.

Writing ability. Clear writing is essential to most careers, especially those in administration and management. Engage your students in writing tasks and emphasize its importance. Your institution might offer writing programs; if so, be sure that they address the special needs and contexts of technical writing. If they don't, lobby for such a program—or start one yourself. There are many resources that can help you do this.

Oral communication. Speaking is at least as important as writing. Students must be able to present ideas and results to other scientists and engineers, as well as to the lay public and specialists in other fields. For students with low confidence, begin with "safe" exercises: Ask them questions and let them respond without interrupting. As they gain confidence, move on to class presentations and talks at student disciplinary-society meetings. Help them develop their research presentations. Videotaping practice sessions can enable students to see correctable habits, and it helps build their confidence. Watching oneself on videotape is often embarrassing; let students watch the tapes in privacy. Many students benefit from professional training, via speech classes or consultation.

Teaching. One of the most important communication skills is teaching, a skill that undergraduates can begin to develop. One way is to accompany them to high schools where the students can offer career guidance and college information. The undergraduate gains a stronger connection with you and becomes an "expert" to the high-school students.

Developing Skills as a Graduate Student

Communication skills. Rather than withdraw into the isolation of research, students should continue to develop their writing ability and oral expression during graduate

BUILDING TRUST

The mentoring relationship might focus on work, but it is fundamentally a *personal relationship* built on trust. There are many ways to build trust and strengthen the relationship:

➤ **Be a "wise and trusted counselor."** For many students, emotional support is crucial; a mentor is one who cares and who is there when needed. Caring can be demonstrated in such routine ways as being on time for meetings, making notes on what you talk about, and referring to those notes before the next meeting.

➤ **Don't try to over-direct a student.** *Too much help can hinder a student's progress.* Unless the student learns to do the fixing, nothing is gained.

➤ **Look for the "real" problem.** A student with a truly urgent problem might cover it with small talk. Give important issues time to emerge.

➤ **Encourage feedback.** Remind students that you have to understand their needs in order to help. Ask whether you are sufficiently—or too—involved.

➤ **Be direct.** At times, a good mentor must take steps that cause pain. You might decide that a student cannot do the work, despite the best efforts of both of you. Explain your concerns directly and recommend a change.

➤ **Talk at a good time.** If a student approaches you at an inconvenient moment, suggest an alternative time instead of listening impatiently.

➤ **Watch for depression.** Fatigue, pessimism, isolation, and difficulty in concentrating can indicate major depression, which can lead to inability to function and even suicide. Keep handy the telephone number of a counselor or resource person. Be prepared to walk the student across campus yourself if necessary.

➤ **Remember the goal.** Your objective is not to produce "another you." It is to help a person achieve a satisfying education and professional career—and become an effective mentor to future students.

TIPS

years. If they are teaching assistants, they might learn more from leading class discussions than simply grading papers. Use laboratory and other meetings, journal clubs, and department seminars as opportunities for presentations, brainstorming, and group critiques. Eventually they should present posters or papers at national society meetings.

Teaching. Graduate students should have regular practice in communicating their ideas. Universities, industries, and other employers place great importance on instructional skill and the ability to communicate ideas. Graduate students can work with their teaching center, give laboratory seminars, and teach or tutor undergraduates. A senior student can gain excellent experience in mentoring a junior student in a laboratory context, taking some responsibility for the student's progress. Encourage them to design teaching material of their own. *Attend teaching events and offer feedback.*

Grant proposals. Practice in writing grant proposals, like teaching, must begin early. Suggest practical exercises, such as applying for funds to attend a professional meeting or perform an independent research project. As students gain experience, they will be able to provide productive help with your own proposals.

Skills for All Levels

Nonacademic abilities. Most jobs require skills that do not appear in the core curriculum. These skills—such as administration, management, planning, and budgeting— can sometimes be developed through elective courses, temporary jobs, or off-campus internships. Students can benefit from *multiple credentials* (i.e., a second degree, nonmajor courses, or nonacademic skills) when preparing for a career.

A Nurse Who Became a Research Manager

As a single mother of two, Diana Garcia-Prichard worked as a nurse to support her family. But when she signed up for chemistry courses at California State University at Hayward, she felt her life shift. "Physical science was perfectly suited to my thought processes," she says. "It was the first time in my life that I found something *I* really wanted to do."

She completed her BS cum laude, entered graduate school at the University of Rochester, and in 4.5 years had a master's and a PhD in chemical physics. She was hired as a research scientist by Eastman Kodak Company, where she is a senior research scientist who also supervises technology-development projects.

"In grad school I knew I wanted to do research, and I thought I would become a professor and help my community back home in California. But my adviser told me it was too difficult for women to get grants or academic jobs. I didn't have the experience to know there were grants for minorities, and my adviser didn't know it. Fortunately I've had a wonderful research experience here. And Kodak, being a big company, has been able to support some of my other goals."

Dr. Garcia-Prichard has worked hard to reform science policy and education, serving on the Clinton-Gore transition team, the National Science Foundation Education and Human Resources Directorate, an American

continued

PROFILE

Chemical Society editorial board, and the board of a local community college.

"I want students today to be better informed than I was about careers. For example, they need to know what kinds of grants there are and who can get them. Also, there's a huge gap between what students learn in universities and what's needed in an industrial workplace. Here I work in physical chemistry, but I also have to be able to collaborate with materials scientists, engineers, and chemists.

"And they should know that the corporate environment is changing today. Shareholders are forcing corporations to downsize staff, but the work still has to get done.

"Choosing the right adviser can help—someone who not only is a good scientist, but is savvy about careers and understands what you need. If you pick a famous scientist who is not a good caregiver, you end up staying in school too long and doing a lot of their work. I was done in 4.5 years, and part of the reason was that I stood up to my adviser. I told him, if you want someone to do your laboratory work, you'll have to find someone else. I'm here for a chemistry degree, not a degree in plumbing."

Of course, that bold approach will not always be successful. The best advice for students in dealing with their advisers is to be honest, persistent, and communicative. Because the student's goals are not usually the same as those of an adviser, a good relationship requires continued effort, good judgment, and good will—on both sides.

> **PROFILE**

People skills. Discourage students from working in isolation from others. People skills—the abilities to listen, to share ideas, and to express oneself—are indispensable for most positions. Look for opportunities to include shy or withdrawn students in social gatherings and group projects. Excessive shyness could be a symptom of more-serious personal problems, for which you might want to suggest counseling.

Leadership. Advise students to join and take a leadership role in disciplinary societies, journal clubs, student government, class exercises, and volunteer activities.

Teamwork. Learning is often most effective within a community of scholars. Cooperative problem-solving skills can be developed through group exercises, collaborative laboratory work, and other team projects. Team skills have gained importance with the trend toward multidisciplinary work in science and engineering.

Creative thinking. A productive scientist or engineer is one who approaches problems with an open mind. Give students permission to move beyond timid or conventional solutions and remind them that original thinking carries some risk. Provide an environment where it is safe to take intellectual risks.

For a list of personal skills and attributes that are helpful to scientists and engineers, see appendix B in COSEPUP's *Careers in Science and Engineering: A Student Planning Guide to Grad School and Beyond.*

Summary Points

➤ **Undergraduates:** Be alert for students with poor work habits or communication skills. Design classroom and laboratory assignments to develop those skills. When necessary, suggest speech classes or consultations.

➤ **Graduate students:** At the graduate level, students can hone their writing and speaking skills by leading discussions, giving presentations, and presenting posters or papers. They should also practice teaching, mentoring, and writing grant proposals.

➤ **All students:** Encourage students at all levels to develop skills that will allow them to advance to positions of greater responsibility, such as management, administration, and budgeting. Such skills might be gained during summer or temporary jobs.

➤ **All students:** Help students find opportunities to develop people skills, leadership, teamwork, and creative thinking; these skills could mean the difference between an average career and an outstanding one.

5

THE MENTOR AS ROLE MODEL

In a good mentoring relationship, you, as the senior partner, can be a role model through both your words and your actions. By who you are, you provide a personal window for the student on a possible future. Your ethical, scientific, and professional behavior all leave a strong impression on students, as does your attitude toward your work.

Communicate your feelings about your professional career. Share your frustrations as well as your enthusiasms. When something excites you, tell your students why. Communicate the importance of mentoring and your hope that students will some day be mentors themselves.

A student might see or understand only a part of what you do—probably your scientific or engineering activities. Take the time to raise other topics that you are comfortable in discussing with your students. What is a typical day, week, or weekend like for you? What does it feel like to do what you do? You might want to talk about administrative, entrepreneurial, or civic activities; family obligations or the

A Geneticist-Molecular Biologist
Who Became a Patent Lawyer

Rochelle Karen Seide, who was educated as a biologist, now enjoys a rewarding career as a patent attorney specializing in biotechnology. After beginning her studies in bacteriology and earning a PhD in human genetics, she completed her schooling with a law degree. This seemingly radical career change, she says, came naturally enough as an extension of her inborn people skills.

"Even when I was a scientist [at Northeastern Ohio Universities College of Medicine], I spent a lot of time with other people teaching and doing genetic counseling. I liked the interpersonal aspects of my work as well as the science. Patent practice lets me use them both."

Dr. Seide became an attorney in the New York firm of Brumbaugh, Graves, Donohue & Raymond. In her specialty of intellectual-property law, she spends much of her time in litigation and counseling: Does a new biotechnology process or product merit a patent? Can a client expect good protection for the life of the patent? To answer such questions, she must understand the cutting-edge research that her clients are doing. She could not do this without her expertise in—and love for—science.

Dr. Seide feels that it was important to focus on science for its own sake while working toward her PhD. Still, she encourages students to understand that "if you want to do science from another perspective, more avenues are open to you. I have found how exciting it is to learn from people in other disciplines and to look at science from other perspectives."

PROFILE

challenge of a dual-career partnership; and your goal of balancing the professional and personal aspects of life.

The sum of all those activities—of all your actions as a mentor—is what students take with them after graduation. The image of you as a person will last longer than your words or professional achievements. The power and value of the image will depend on the efforts you have made in building honesty, trust, and good communication throughout your mentoring relationship.

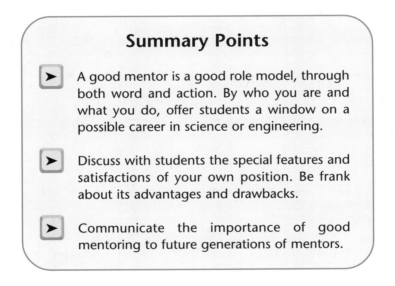

Summary Points

> A good mentor is a good role model, through both word and action. By who you are and what you do, offer students a window on a possible career in science or engineering.

> Discuss with students the special features and satisfactions of your own position. Be frank about its advantages and drawbacks.

> Communicate the importance of good mentoring to future generations of mentors.

6

RECOMMENDATION: IMPROVING THE QUALITY OF MENTORING

In this guide, we have listed many steps that individual faculty members and senior students can take to become more-effective mentors. However, the effectiveness of mentoring at every level is partly a function of institutional support. According to a report by the Council of Graduate Schools, "Universities, graduate schools, and departments all can play prominent parts in fostering mentorship among faculty members."

Institutions have a large stake in promoting effective mentoring at the undergraduate, graduate, postdoctoral, and junior-faculty levels. As we have suggested in this guide, improved mentoring is likely to enhance students' educational experience, morale, career planning and placement, and professional competence.

The most direct way for institutions to improve the quality of mentoring is to reward good mentoring. Faculty members at research-oriented institutions are often rewarded for good research but seldom for good mentoring; in fact, faculty might actually be penalized for mentoring to the extent that time devoted to students is time not spent on research.

Unless good mentoring is embedded in institutional systems of rewards and promotions, it is unfair to expect faculty members to assign high priority to good mentoring. Therefore, *we recommend that institutions incorporate mentoring and advising effectiveness in the criteria used for appraisals of faculty performance, including evaluations for the purposes of promotion and tenure.*

Few institutions have developed mechanisms for appraising mentoring performance. Because techniques of mentoring vary widely among individuals (including the amount of time spent with students, the degree of intervention in student choices, how meetings with students are structured, and the extent of joint activities), qualitative measures are of little value. Given the logical premise that one's mentoring effectiveness is reflected by the later achievements of one's students, however, a number of useful mechanisms for appraising mentoring performance are apparent. For example, institutions could

➤ Track the progress of former students to provide information about the career experiences of graduates.

➤ Develop a faculty evaluation form and ask third-year graduate students to complete it, assessing how well their mentors (or other faculty members) have contributed to their research, scholarship, and general education. A sample form is available at the NRC Web site: http://www.nap.edu/readingroom/books/mentor.

➤ Collect data from current students on their perceptions of faculty performance in mentoring and advising.

In addition to appraising mentoring performance, institutions can take other steps to stimulate better mentoring, including the following:

➤ Take a more active role in choosing faculty advisers to ensure that those with good mentoring ability are included.

➤ Provide guidance on mentoring for new faculty and advisers, which can include briefings, workshops, the assignment of senior mentors, and instructions on campus and Internet resources. Periodic seminars can be held where senior faculty describe good mentoring and junior faculty ask questions; this guide can be used as a resource.

➤ Provide discipline-oriented career counselors who can offer students and advisers up-to-date information on the full range of educational and career opportunities for scientists and engineers, including industrial internships, combined degrees, part-time and summer placements, and classes outside their discipline.

➤ Sponsor more discussions of topics relevant to mentoring, such as professional standards, ethical values, balancing career and personal life, and finding a good postdoctoral student.

➤ Offer students a "guide to mentors" describing their responsibilities and those of mentors and including relevant descriptions of potential mentors and achievements of mentors' former students.

➤ Monitor abuses of power by faculty—through departmental oversight, student evaluations, time-to-degree data, and student performance—and include such abuses in the criteria used for faculty evaluation.

➤ Hold annual seminars that update faculty on the latest employment trends, internship opportunities, etc., as well as issues such as appropriate faculty-student relations, cultural and ethnic issues, etc.

➤ Develop requirements for electives and other classes that will broaden the skills and versatility of students.

➤ Create an institutional award for distinguished mentors. The White House Office of Science and Technology Policy and the American Association for the Advancement of Science have recently instituted such awards on the national level. Recognition at the institutional level is a key first step.

Specific techniques of enhancing and rewarding good mentoring must vary by institution. The purpose of this document is not to prescribe techniques, but to encourage a renewed commitment to mentoring at every level. We believe that such a commitment will bring personal as well as professional and institutional rewards to all members of the educational enterprise as they prepare the nation's next generation of scientists and engineers.

RESOURCES

You can mentor more easily and effectively if you know what resources are available at your own institution. A departmental adviser might supply students' schedules and requirements. A student-affairs office usually offers tutoring and workshops on study skills or "college survival." The health or counseling center can usually suggest an appropriate counselor, physician, or psychologist when a student needs professional help with personal problems. To equip yourself to do career planning, begin with your career-placement center, which should have a variety of services and information.

Internet Resources

The Internet can also help you mentor more effectively and easily in a number of ways. For example, e-mail and "chat groups" can be used to keep in touch with students. In addition, the Internet can provide access to worldwide resources, such as those described below.

GOOD MENTORING:
BREAKING THROUGH RED TAPE

A good student at a community college tells his mentor that he must drop out of school because the financial-aid office has not approved his request for a loan. The mentor suspects an error. Having met the financial-aid director, she calls him and sets up an appointment for the student. The next day, the student returns to her office, wearing a smile of success. A new person in the financial-aid office has overlooked the kind of loan that applies to his case.

Comment: Knowing the right person to call can save time for the mentor and avoid trouble for the student. When you find helpful resource persons anywhere on campus, note their names. Such a list could be the key to solving the next problem. Also, keep a copy of the student handbook and the requirements for a degree in your office.

STYLES

The Committee on Science, Engineering, and Public Policy's (COSEPUP) homepage (http://www2.nas.edu/cosepup) has links to on-line versions of its useful resources *Reshaping the Graduate Education of Scientists and Engineers, Careers in Science and Engineering: A Student Planning Guide to Grad School and Beyond, On Being a Scientist: Responsible Conduct in Research,* and *A National Conversation on Doctoral Education: An Emerging Consensus.*

Two key Internet resources are: The National Research Council's *Career Planning Center for Beginning Scientists and Engineers* (CPC) (http://www2.nas.edu/cpc) and the American Association for the Advancement of Science (AAAS) *Science's NextWave* (http://www.nextwave.org). The CPC includes a bulletin board, an on-line mentoring center, data on trends and changes in the job market, and links to the many useful on-line books, job and research funding listings, and disciplinary society web sites. The NextWave has open forums on topical issues, feature articles on alternative science careers, site reviews, news articles, and nuts-and-bolts science career advice columns.

Gender, Cultural, and Disability Issues

Minority-group students can obtain guidance and scholarship aid through NACME, Empire State Building, 350 Fifth Ave., Suite 2212, New York, NY 10118-2299 (Telephone, 212/279-2626; URL, http://www.nacme.org). The New England Board of Higher Education also has materials of value for minority-group and other students (45 Temple Place, Boston, MA 02111; Telephone, 617/357-9620; Fax, 617/338-1577; URL, http://www.nebhe.org). Remember, however, that e-mail is not always confidential.

A number of organizations focus on gender-related issues. Two key organizations are the Association of Women in Science (http://www.awis.org) and the Society of Women Engineers (http://www.swe.org). They should be able to provide guidance or point you toward a related discipline-specific organization.

Students with disabilities may obtain guidance from the following organizations:

➤ Association on Higher Education and Disability (AHEAD); 614/488–4972. Promotes education, communication, and training.

➤ Educational Resources Information Center (ERIC); 800/848–4815. A focus on disability issues.

➤ Higher Education and Adult Training for the Handicapped (HEATH), now renamed for Persons with Disabilities); 800/544–3284, 202/939–9320. Helps with transitions from high school to college, college to graduate school.

➤ Job Accommodation Network (JAN); 800/526–7234. How persons with a disability can be accommodated in the laboratory or workplace.

➤ National Information Center on Deafness; 202/451–5051. Resources for deaf and hearing-impaired students.

➤ President's Committee on Employment of People with Disabilities; 202/376–6200; www.pcepd.gov. Excellent reference source, with liaison person in each state.

Bibliography

For additional material, see the bibliography in the COSEPUP guide *Careers in Science and Engineering: A Student Planning Guide to Grad School and Beyond* (http://www2.nas.edu/cosepup).

Doing Science

Beveridge, W.I.B. 1950. *The Art of Scientific Investigation.* United States: Vintage Books.

Committee on Science, Engineering, and Public Policy. 1995. *On Being a Scientist: Responsible Conduct in Research.* Washington, D.C.: National Academy Press.

Medawar, P.B. 1979. *Advice to a Young Scientist.* United States: Basic Books.

Peters, R.L. 1996. *Getting What You Came For: The Smart Student's Guide to Earning a Master's or a PhD.* New York: Farrar, Straus, and Giroux.

Presentations

Briscoe, M.H. 1995. *Preparing Scientific Illustrations: A Guide to Better Posters, Presentations, and Publications.* New York: Springer-Verlag.

Job-Hunting

Bolles, R.N. 1997. *The 1997 What Color Is Your Parachute?* Berkeley, Calif.: Ten Speed Press.

Committee on Science, Engineering, and Public Policy. 1996. *Careers in Science and Engineering: A Student Planning Guide to Grad School and Beyond.* Washington, D.C.: National Academy Press.

Hirsch, A. 1996. *Interviewing: A National Business Employment Weekly Premier Guide.* 2nd edition. New York: Wiley and Sons.

Schwartz, B.B. ed. 1994. *Graduate Student Packet for Students in Physics.* College Park, Md. APS (American Physical Society) and AIP (American Institute of Physics).

Yate, M. 1996. *Knock 'Em Dead: The Ultimate Job Seeker's Handbook.* Holbrook, Mass.: Adams Media Corp.

Mentoring

Association for Women in Science. 1993. *Mentoring Means Future Scientists.* Washington, D.C.: Association for Women in Science.

Audi, R. 1994. "On the ethics of teaching and the ideals of learning," *Academe,* September–October: 27–36.

Bird, S.J. 1994. "Overlooked aspects in the education of science professionals: Mentoring, ethics, and professional responsibility." *J. Science Education and Technology* 3:49–55.

Council of Graduate Schools. 1990. *Research Student and Supervisor: An Approach to Good Supervisory Practice.* Washington, D.C.: Council of Graduate Schools.

_____. 1995. *A Conversation About Mentoring: Trends and Models.* Washington, D.C.: Council of Graduate Schools.

Fort, C., Bird, S.J., and Didion, C.J. (eds.) 1993. *A Hand Up: Women Mentoring Women in Science.* Washington, D.C.: Association for Women in Science.

Kanigel, R. 1986. *Apprentice to Genius: The Making of a Scientific Dynasty.* Baltimore, Md.: Johns Hopkins University Press.

Olmstead, M.A. 1993. "Mentoring new faculty: Advice to department chairs," *CSWP, A Newsletter of the Committee on the Status of Women in Physics,* Vol. 13, No. 1: 1, 8–11. Washington, D.C.: American Physical Society, August.

Noe, R.A. 1988. "An investigation of the determinants of successful assigned mentoring," *Personnel Psychology* 41:457–479.

Roberts, G.C. and Sprague, R.L. 1995. "To compete or to educate? Mentoring and the research climate," *Professional Ethics Report VIII*, 1:6–7, Fall.

Zelditch, M. 1990. "Mentor roles," in *Proceedings of the 32nd Annual Meeting of the Western Association of Graduate Schools,* 11. Tempe, Ariz., March 16–18.

Oral Communication

Schloff, L. and Yudkin, M. 1992. *Smart Speaking.* New York: Plume.

Stuart, C. 1989. *How to Be an Effective Speaker.* Chicago: NTC Publishing Group.

Time Management and Professional Development

Griessman, B.E. 1994. *Time Tactics of Very Successful People.* New York: McGraw-Hill.

Hobfoll, S.E. and Hobfoll, I.H. 1994. *Work Won't Love You Back: The Dual Career Couple's Survival Guide.* New York: W.H. Freeman.

Roesch, R. 1996. *The Working Woman's Guide to Managing Time.* Englewood Cliffs, NJ: Prentice Hall.

Gender, Cultural, and Disability Issues

Association for Women in Science. 1995. *A Hand Up: Women Mentoring Women in Science,* 2nd edition. Washington, DC.

Didion, C.J. 1993. "Letters of reference: an often-deciding factor in women's academic or career advancement." *Journal of College Science Teaching* 23 (1): 9–10.

Katz, M. and Vieland, V. 1993. *Get Smart! What You Should Know (But Won't Learn in Class) About Sexual Harassment and Sexual Discrimination.* New York: The Feminist Press, City University of New York.

Mitchell, R. 1993. *The Multicultural Student's Guide to Colleges.* New York: Noonday Press.

National Research Council. 1989. *A Common Destiny: Blacks and American Society.* Washington, D.C.: National Academy Press.

National Science Foundation. 1996. *Women, Minorities, and Persons with Disabilities in Science and Engineering.* Washington, D.C.: National Science Foundation.

Rosser, S.V. 1990. *Female-Friendly Science: Applying Women's Studies Methods and Theories to Attract Students.* New York: Pergamon Press.

Sonnert, G. and Holton, G. 1995. *Who Succeeds in Science? The Gender Dimension.* New Brunswick, N.J.: Rutgers University Press.

Treisman, U. 1992. "Studying students studying calculus: A look at the lives of minority mathematics students in college," *College Mathematics Journal* 23 (5):362–72, November.

Responsible Scientific Conduct

Committee on Science, Engineering, and Public Policy. 1995. *On Being a Scientist: Responsible Conduct on Research,* 2nd edition. Washington, D.C.: National Academy Press.

Elliott, D. and Stern, J.E., eds. 1997. *Research Ethics: A Reader.* Hanover, N.H.: University Press of New England.

Korenman, S.G. and Shipp, A., eds. 1994. *Teaching the Responsible Conduct of Research through a Case Study Approach: A Handbook for Instructors.* Washington, D.C.: Association of American Medical Colleges.

Macrina, F.L. 1995. *Scientific Integrity: An Introductory Text with Cases.* Washington, D.C.: ASM Press.

Sigma Xi. 1986. *Honor in Science.* Research Triangle Park, North Carolina: Sigma Xi.

"Special Issue on Research Ethics." 1995. *Professional Ethics,* Vol. 4, Nos. 3 & 4, Spring/Summer.

Stern, J.E. and Elliott, D. 1997. *The Ethics of Scientific Research: A Guidebook for Course Development.* Hanover, N.H.: University Press of New England.

Teaching

Committee on Science, Engineering, and Public Policy. 1995. *Reshaping the Graduate Education of Scientists and Engineers.* Washington, D.C.: National Academy Press.

Committee on Science, Engineering, and Public Policy. 1996. *A National Conversation on Doctoral Education: An Emerging Consensus.* Washington, D.C.: COSEPUP.

McKeachie, W.J. 1994. *Teaching Tips: A Guidebook for the Beginning College Teacher,* 9th edition. Lexington, Mass.: D.C. Heath and Co.

Pregent, R. 1994. *Charting Your Course: How to Prepare to Teach More Effectively.* Madison, Wisc.: Magna Publications.

Writing

Booth, V. 1993. *Communicating in Science: Writing a Scientific Paper and Speaking at Scientific Meetings,* 2nd edition. New York: Cambridge University Press.

Council of Biology Editors, Committee on Graduate Training in Scientific Writing. 1968. *Scientific Writing for Graduate Students: A Manual on the Teaching of Scientific Writing.* New York: Rockefeller University Press.

Day, R.A. 1994. *How to Write and Publish a Scientific Paper,* 4th edition. Phoenix: Oryx Press.

Moriarty, M.E. 1997. *Writing Science Through Critical Thinking.* New York: Jones and Bartlett.

REPORT BRIEF

RESHAPING THE GRADUATE EDUCATION OF SCIENTISTS AND ENGINEERS

COMMITTEE ON SCIENCE, ENGINEERING,
AND PUBLIC POLICY

The graduate education of scientists and engineers—an activity of growing importance in an increasingly technological world—must change to reflect developments in science, engineering, the economy, and the broader society. With more than half of new PhDs going to work in nonacademic settings, graduate education needs to impart a broader range of skills. At the same time, the PhD should retain the features, including an original research experience, that have made it a world model.

The result of these changes, writes the Committee on Science, Engineering, and Public Policy in its report *Reshaping the Graduate Education of Scientists and Engineers*, would be a new kind of PhD, one that emphasizes adaptability and versatility as well as technical proficiency. COSEPUP, a joint committee of the National Academy of Sciences, the National Academy of Engineering, and the Institute of Medicine, recommends that graduate programs provide a broader exposure to experiences desired by both academic and nonacademic employers. Faculty and institutions also should offer better career information and guidance to students so that they can make well-informed decisions in planning their academic and professional careers. Graduate education should prepare students for an increasingly interdisciplinary, collaborative, and global job market and should not be viewed only as a byproduct of immersion in an intensive research experience. The primary objective of graduate education should be the education of students.

The changing job market. Scientists and engineers with PhDs and other advanced degrees play a central and growing role in American industrial and commercial life. They contribute directly to the national goals of technological, economic, and cultural development—not only as researchers and educators but in a wide variety of other professional roles. And as the country responds to expanded economic competition, urgent public health needs, environmental degradation, new national security challenges, and other pressing issues, a widening variety of professions and organizations are hiring the approximately 25,000 people who receive a PhD each year (up from about 18,000 a decade ago).

But a mismatch between the numbers of new PhDs and traditional research-oriented jobs in academia has led to considerable frustration and disappointment among young scientists and engineers. Fewer than one-third of those who received PhDs in science and engineering in 1983-86 were in tenure track positions or had tenure in 1991. New PhDs are spending more time as postdoctoral fellows while they wait for permanent jobs to become available. Downsizing and restructuring in industry and government also have reduced the number of jobs focused on basic research in those sectors.

Despite the difficulties finding jobs in basic research, hiring in other areas has been vigorous enough to keep the overall unemployment level of PhDs relatively low. An increasing number of doctorate recipients are doing applied research, development, and management in industry, working in government or nonprofit institutions, or teaching in elementary and secondary schools.

A new PhD. COSEPUP found a common theme in its examination of the job market for PhDs. Many future job opportunities will favor students with a greater breadth of academic and career skills than graduate students typically acquire today. The committee therefore recommended a new model of PhD education that incorporates the following changes:

➤ **More versatility**. Graduate programs, especially at the departmental level, should provide options that allow students to gain a wider variety of academic and career skills. Students who intend to seek a career in basic research should have a grounding in the broad fundamentals of their fields and should have some personal familiarity with several subfields. In addition, experiences that supply career skills beyond those gained in the classroom and laboratory, such as off-campus internships, could make graduates more effective in business, government, and academia at all levels. Many institutions have been experimenting with such innovations, providing a rich array of reproducible models.

Employers in all sectors value the requirement for original research that is the hallmark of the PhD. Hybrid degrees that do not involve such research have not been successful in the past. But a student interested in working in nontraditional fields should have the option to design a dissertation

To foster the new model of PhD education recommended by COSEPUP, colleges and universities and their faculties should:

➤ Give students more options in pursuing the PhD.

➤ Provide a broader educational experience through such mechanisms as internships or minor degrees.

➤ Provide better career guidance and job placement to entering and graduating students.

➤ Control the time to degree.

that meets high standards for originality but is more flexible in terms of time required, subject matter treated, and approach taken.

➤ **Better career information and guidance**. The lack of accurate, timely, and accessible data on employment trends, careers, and sources of student support is a serious flaw in the graduate education system. A national database that covers such issues as financial aid, time to degree, and placement rates—including information gathered and disseminated through the Internet—could help students and their advisers make informed decisions about professional careers.

➤ **Less time to degree**. The median number of years between receipt of a bachelors degree and a PhD in science and engineering has risen to more than 8 years, an increase of about 2 years since 1960. The reasons for this increase are largely unknown, but some of it may be a result of students working as highly specialized research assistants or as teaching assistants in ways that do not directly contribute to their

Students should:

➤ Obtain, before entering a graduate school, information on the employment pattern of the school's graduates.

➤ Pursue an education that provides a broad range of experiences.

➤ Press advisors for information on career options and realistic employment expectations.

education. Each institution should set its own standards for time to degree and enforce them.

➤ **Education/training grants**. The heavy reliance on research assistantships for graduate student support has tended to make the needs of research projects rather than the students' educational needs paramount. Education/ training grants awarded competitively to institutions and departments that emphasize adapt-ability and breadth could help develop and sustain locally developed programs.

COSEPUP saw no reason to recommend limits on enrollments or on the number of foreign students in graduate programs. Greater flexibility and more information in graduate programs will enhance the system's ability to mesh with the job market. And these changes, combined with better precollege education, will attract more American students to graduate education—particularly women and minorities, who remain seriously underrepresented in some fields of science and engineering.

A shift in perspective. In the past, graduate schools typically have seen their mission as producing the next genera-

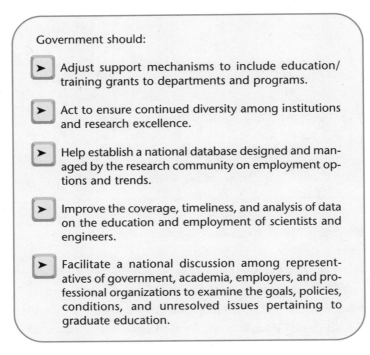

Government should:

➤ Adjust support mechanisms to include education/ training grants to departments and programs.

➤ Act to ensure continued diversity among institutions and research excellence.

➤ Help establish a national database designed and managed by the research community on employment options and trends.

➤ Improve the coverage, timeliness, and analysis of data on the education and employment of scientists and engineers.

➤ Facilitate a national discussion among representatives of government, academia, employers, and professional organizations to examine the goals, policies, conditions, and unresolved issues pertaining to graduate education.

tion of academic researchers. But scientists and engineers now contribute to national needs in many other ways. To contribute most effectively to the need for highly trained scientists and engineers, graduate schools need to review their missions and consider new approaches. If they do so, graduate education could play an even more important role in society than it has played in the past.

For more information, including an on-line version of the full text of the report, visit the COSEPUP homepage at http://www2.nas.edu/cosepup.